MORE WALKS IN WARKS

MORE WALKS IN WARKS

Julie M Chiswick

ISBN 10:1508844461
ISBN 13: 9781508844464

About the Author

Julie Chiswick has lived with her husband in a bustling village in Warwickshire for the past 30 years. They have one daughter and walking has always been an enjoyable hobby for all the family.

She taught in primary schools and for many years taught English to adult students in the borough of Solihull and surrounding areas.

This is her second book of walks.

To learn more of Julie, visit her website www.juliechiswick.co.uk

Foreword

Following the success of *Walks in Warks* (many thanks to those who bought it) I decided to publish this second book.

The walks in this book have been an interesting challenge. More than two-thirds are totally new and planned carefully using the OS Explorer Map series. The rest are 'old' walks which have been revised and re-worked owing to many changes. Over the years properties disappear, new ones appear, stiles are replaced by kissing gates and routes become disused or impassable. Eighteen of these walks were undertaken in 2014 and the last three in early Spring 2015 so they are completely up to date at the time of publication.

Julie Chiswick

April 2015

To my dear Mum, whose favourite pastime was walking

Contents

Symbols used in this book

This book uses symbols to highlight certain paragraphs and point out useful information.

 Take care or be aware at this point.

 A place or item of interest.

 A resting place for non-alcoholic drinks and light refreshments.

 A place where alcohol and meals are available.

Disclaimer

At the time of publication, all the walks in this book follow public rights of way or permitted paths. The publisher and author cannot be held legally responsible should routes alter owing to diversion orders or other changes. Neither can the publisher and author be held responsible for damage resulting from walkers trespassing on private property either deliberately or inadvertently.

At the time of writing the places and charges for parking are as stated. These may change depending on the policies of the individuals and authorities concerned.

WALK 1: SHUSTOKE RESERVOIR
Distance: 4.5 miles

Parking: Park in the reservoir public car park. No charge at the time of writing.

The walk starts from the reservoir car park off the B4114 in Shustoke village. It is on the left as you approach the village from Coleshill.

A walking stick may be helpful on one section of the walk where there is a lot of undergrowth at certain times of the year.

Julie M Chiswick   1

The Walk

OS Explorer map 232: (Nuneaton and Tamworth)

▶ Walk from the car park towards the sailing club and go through a wooden gate to the right of the club. This leads on to a path through a wooded area running alongside the sailing club. (This short section might be muddy in winter months or after a lot of rain). In the summer months, listen out for a variety of birdsong .

▶ Emerge on to a grassy path crossing a meadow with the reservoir on your left. In the late spring and early summer there are buttercups and wild flowers galore here.

▶ Continue to the end of the meadow and then go across to a tarmac path. Turn left (not straight on over the bridge) along an unmade path for a short distance.

▶ As you reach the set of wooden gates at the end, turn right over a metal footbridge and up some brick steps to the small reservoir on your right. Fishing is allowed here.

▶ Continue round on the track to the railway line at the end. At the **Circular Walk** signpost, turn right to walk alongside the railway line.

▶ As the narrow track turns 90 degrees right, you must go left over the railway line at a metal gate.

▶ Continue straight ahead. This section can be very full of wild flowers, greenery and some nettles in spring and summer, so use your stick if necessary to make your way along. Ahead you will see a house. This is where you are heading, to the main road.

▶ When you reach the road, turn right and walk along the verge passing the **Over Whitacre** sign. Pass **The Firs** on the right and then cross over the road to the footpath and turn left at **Botts Green Road**. Part way along here you will pass an unusual gated property on your right called **Kameruka**. Keep going and at the junction turn right and then immediately right over a partially hidden stile into a small copse.

▶ Exit the copse into a field and go across this field to a stile on the other side.

▶ Cross this stile into another field with a large house with an indoor swimming pool called **Stone Bank** (worth a photo) on your right . Head across the field to skirt the house and up to the road. In the corner at the end of the house is a high stile. Exit here on to the road.

Stone Bank

▶ Turn left down the road. This is the hamlet of **Botts Green**. You will soon pass the entrance to **Botts Green Hall** on your right (a black and white timbered building). It is a grade 11 listed building dating back to 1593. You may be able to get a glimpse if you go a little way up the path from the road.

▶ Continue to the junction up ahead and take the road left signposted **Kingsbury**. Pass a house called **The Counting House** on your right and then the road goes through a shaded area of overhanging trees.

▶ At the next junction, keep to the right signposted Kingsbury again. Keep walking and you will see the houses of **Nether Whitacre** ahead and to the right.

▶ Continue to the main road (which can be quite busy). Go left, keeping on the grass verge as much as possible. This stretch is only a few hundred yards.

▶ As the main road bends left, you must cross over into **Hoggrills End Lane** and continue along here for a short way until you reach **Hill Farm** and the barn conversions on your right. Opposite these houses go through the metal kissing gate into a field. The reservoir can be seen in the distance.

▶ Continue diagonally left downhill towards the railway line, passing through another metal kissing gate at the bottom of the field. Go through a gate, under the railway arch and up steps onto a narrow path.

▶ Turn left for 100 yards or so and then go right by the waymarker. (You will recognise this small section from earlier in the walk).

▶ Continue down the steps, over the metal footbridge and up the next steps, turning right to complete your walk round the other side of the reservoir. Follow round the reservoir and if you wish to stop, there are seats at the far end. Continue all the way round and at the metal pier and wooden gate, exit the reservoir, turning right towards the car park.

 Refreshments and food can be found at **The Plough Inn**, which is on the main road almost opposite the turning to the reservoir car park.

Shustoke Reservoir

Points of Interest:

The **two reservoirs** at Shustoke are owned by Severn Trent Water. The water to fill the reservoirs is drawn from the River Bourne, which runs to the north. It is then pumped to Whitacre Water Works where it is treated and piped to Nuneaton and Coventry. The reservoirs are well known for some unusual birdlife. In the spring their banks are covered in cowslips, celandines and other wild flowers. The reservoirs are conveniently situated on the North Warwickshire Cycle Way and cycle racks are provided near to the car park.

St Cuthbert's, Shustoke's parish church, was erected in 1307 on the site of an earlier church or chapel. Remains of a Celtic churchyard cross and reused Norman masonry are in evidence. The parish registers are among the earliest in the country and date from the reign of Henry VIII.

Julie M Chiswick

WALK 2: BADDESLEY CLINTON
Distance: 5 miles

Parking: Park in Baddesley Clinton House car park. No charge.
There are toilets close by the visitor centre.

This is a gentle walk on lanes and in fields, past Rowington Church and
along the canal via Kingswood Junction and back to Baddesley Clinton
grounds.

The Walk

OS Explorer map 221 and OS Explorer map 220 (Birmingham south side)

▶ Leave the car park at the far end by a gate on the right hand side.

St Michael' s

 ▶ Turn left and follow the path to **St Michael's Church** on your left. It is usually open and well worth a visit.

▶ Continue on the path a short way, turning right by the blue bridleway sign into a field. Keep to the hedge on your left and go through a metal gate into another field with a mound on your left and a wooden circular feature.

▶ Take the metal gate on the left into another field – this time with the hedge on your right. At the far end go through a gate on to a lane and

Julie M Chiswick   7

continue straight ahead. After a while bear left at the blue bridleway signs. The path goes past farm barns, a farmhouse and a long red brick wall on your right.

▶ Exit by a gate to the road. Turn right and almost immediately left into **Queen's Drive**, with the cricket pitch on the right. You pass a few large houses on the left and then the road continues with greenery on either side. You will soon meet the main road ahead.

▶ Cross the road and turn left. (You may notice an interesting gate with the name **The Elephant and Castle** on it.) Continue on the footpath a short distance into **Rowington**.

▶ Go ahead and you will soon see the church of **St Laurence** on your left, raised from the road. (It is thought the present stone church was built in the 12th century). The village hall is on your right, the **Old** Vicarage on the left just before the church.

▶ As the road bends sharply left at the church, you must take a lane on the right following a row of red brick walls. The lane soon arrives at the **Grand Union Canal**. Go over the bridge and drop down to the right along the towpath, with the canal on your right.

▶ Walk for about 15 minutes until you arrive at bridge 63 (**Turner's Green**). On your left just before the bridge is an information board and an interesting winding box telling the *Idle Women* story. Do have a listen! Might be a good place for that flask of coffee too.

▶ Continue under the bridge heading towards **Kingswood Junction** where the **Stratford Canal** joins from the left. This section is about a 10 minute walk along the towpath.

▶ Go over the bridge at Kingswood Junction and continue for a few minutes to bridge 65. Go up the steps and turn right past **The Navigation** pub.

▶ After about 100 yards you take a left turn at a well signposted track which goes past a barn conversion on your right and continues through

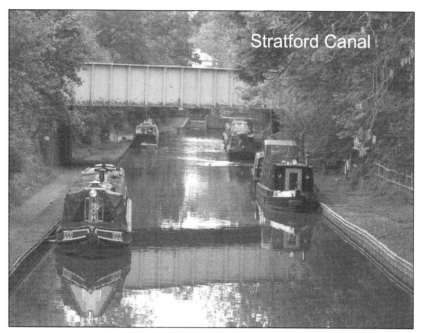

Stratford Canal

a metal gate into a stable yard. The track goes out across fields with a fence-protected walkway.

► Go through a metal gate into a large field and keep straight ahead.

► Exit this field over a tiny bridge and gate and continue across the fields (often plenty of sheep here) until you reach the main driveway of **Baddesley Clinton House**. If you have time do visit the house as it's very interesting.

► Turn right and walk back to the car park.

Refreshments can be had at **The Navigation** we passed en route in Lapworth, the **Orange Tree** at **Chadwick End** or the **King's Arms** (until recently the Heron's Nest) if you're travelling towards **Knowle**.

WALK 3: BARSTON LAKES
Distance: 5 miles

Parking: Park in the Bull's Head on Barston Lane. You may wish to call the landlord on 01675 442830 to request his permission.

This walk starts at the Bull's Head in Barston, and passes West Midlands Golf Course and Barston Lakes. It continues round the edge of Hampton in Arden and the hamlet of Walsal End.

The Walk

OS Explorer map 221 (Coventry and Warwick)

▶ Turn left at the main road as you leave the **Bull's Head** pub. Cross over the road and you will pass **Barston Parish Church** on your right. At the end of the houses the footpath ends, so take care as you walk on the road for a short distance.

▶ On your right you will soon pass a tall, crenellated wall with a fine, large house attached to it. Just after this, turn left into **Ryton End**. Follow this quiet country lane for about half a mile.

▶ At the end of this lane you reach a 5-bar metal gate. Go by the side of it and join the bridleway ahead.

▶ Continue along and then bear right. Ahead of you is the **West Midlands Golf Club**. Follow the bridleway all the way round the edge of the

Barston Lakes

driving range.

▶ At the entrance road to the golf club, turn right and then left at the large gates to pick up the path once again.

▶ With the car park on your left, continue along this path and the lake will then be on your left. (It may be busy with fishermen if there is a competition day). You may wish to stop for a coffee break by the side of the lake and take in the scenery.

▶ At the end of the lake the path bends left. Watch out for a bridge on your right. Go over this and follow a narrow path through a wooded nature area.

▶ Just before a metal gate you go left through a small copse at the public footpath sign to **Hampton**.

▶ Exit the trees at a kissing gate and head across the fields and over the next few stiles towards Hampton. Continue straight across and exit through a kissing gate and along a narrow enclosed track to houses.

▶ Continue straight ahead (not right) and opposite the last house on the left turn right through the kissing gate. Go straight ahead (ignoring the kissing gate to your right)! Keep the wire fence and then hedge on your right. At the end of this field go through the kissing gate and up the grassy slope with the fence on your right. This is a steady climb uphill.

▶ As you reach the top you will see the **Beeches Restaurant** and grounds to your left. Exit by a final kissing gate just by the Beeches.

▶ Walk ahead by the side of a house to meet **Marsh Lane** and turn left, walking up to the junction with the **High Street**.

▶ Turn left and after about 20 yards turn left into **Belle Vue Terrace**. Walk down to the bottom and as the road bends right, look for the footpath by a lamppost. It is hidden between hedges. Walk along here and over the stile at the end.

► Turn left down the field heading away from the village. Cross the stile by a gate and to the next stile with the hedge always on your left.

► Go through this field (with large greenhouses over to your right). Cross a wooden bridge over a stream and keep straight through the next long large field with the hedge on your left. You will come to a narrow tarmac farm track at the end.

► Go through the kissing gate and cross the track to go over a tiny bridge and up into the next field. All is well signposted. At this point you will see farm barns to your right. Continue into the next field with a large house over to your right at the top of the field and go up to meet the lane in the hamlet of **Walsal End**.

► Follow the lane left through the hamlet passing some lovely old timbered houses. Be careful here as it's easy to miss the correct path. As the track bends right, you must go slightly left on to the driveway of the old timbered cottage known as **Red Barns**. Then continue straight ahead across the front of the next house and you will see a stile ahead of you.

► Keep going along a rough grassy track which bears left and then right through an opening on to a field. Walk diagonally left across this large field towards a wooden bridge in a small group of trees. (If the field is difficult to walk across, then follow it round the edge and along the bottom to the bridge).

► Continue across the next field towards the stile. Cross the stile at the end and go across the next field towards a stile right by a telegraph pole.

► Turn left over the stile heading towards a metal kissing gate. Continue across the last field before reaching houses. Go through a wooden kissing gate and down a narrow grassy path between houses to meet **Oak Lane**.

► Turn right, then left at the main **Barston Lane**. This will take you through the village and back to the **Bull's Head** on your left.

Points of Interest:

The **Bull's Head** dates back to the 1490s. Originally a staging inn on the old main road between Coventry and Birmingham, the pub boasts Shakespearian links. In Henry IV Part 2, the traveller en route to Sutton Coldfield from Stratford-Upon-Avon stays at the inn at Barston. The pub also houses a priest hole dating back to Cromwellian times.

St. Swithin's, Barston's parish church, dates from 1721 and is built on the site of an earlier church.

Barston village contains several interesting timber-framed and tile-roofed buildings dating from the 16th and 17th centuries.

The Bull's Head

WALK 4: KENILWORTH TOWN
Distance: 4 miles

Parking: Park in the castle car park on the B4103, opposite the Queen and Castle pub. This is free parking at the time of writing but can get busy. There is another parking place further into Kenilworth just past the castle if necessary. Otherwise, you can park at the pub, but it is a paying car park.

This walk takes you round the historic town of Kenilworth starting at the castle, going through the town and Kenilworth Common, finishing in Abbey Fields.

The Walk

OS Explorer map 221 (Coventry and Warwick)

►Exit the car park opposite the houses and pub and cross the road turning left up the hill for a few yards (as safer on the footpath) and then cross back over the road to take the path on your left named **Purlieu Lane.**

Kenilworth Castle

►Just after the thatched cottage on your left, take the signed gap (yellow arrow) by the gate into a large grassy area. Follow the path all the way round keeping the castle walls on your left.

 ►After a short time you will arrive at a kissing gate. After the kissing gate turn right and then almost immediately left up wooden steps. There's a wonderful view of the castle from here and an explanation board about the turreted gateway.

► Continue down some wooden steps and follow the path round, heading left towards the road. You will pass a pond on your right as you approach the road and the car park.

► Exit by a kissing gate and cross the road by the pub and head along **Castle Hill** signposted **Town Centre.**

► You will see the restored thatched cottages of **Little Virginia** on your right. Carry on up Castle Hill passing the end of **Malthouse Lane** and the beginning of **High Street.** There are good views to the right of **Abbey Fields**, which we visit at the end of the walk. Continue along High Street.

High Street

► It's worth taking a look at **St. Nicholas Church,** so look out for a right hand walkway down to the church which is just after the red-brick building named **CONVALESCENT HOME.**

► Retrace your steps to the High Street. Continue along to see some interesting buildings. Just before the traffic lights on the left is **Latimer**

House. Bishop Latimer is said to have preached on the steps there shortly before he went to the stake in Oxford. Next to this is **Milsom's Hotel** dating from the fifteenth century.

▶ Resume the walk by crossing at the traffic lights into **New Street** and proceed for about 350 yards. Soon after the last house on the left is a footpath - almost a bridleway - on the left. This is **Love Lane** and is marked with a yellow arrow.

▶ To the right of this lane is a large field, **Parliament Piece**, gifted to the public in 1987 by Miss Martin of The Spring. It is said that Henry 111 held parliament there in 1266.

▶ After about 200 yards you will see a stile on the right into Parliament Piece. Cross over this and walk diagonally right, heading slightly to the right of a solitary tree. You will see a gate which takes you back on to the road.

▶ Cross the road and go left and then soon on your right take a footpath which goes in front of several houses. The last house on the right is an old windmill now converted into a residence. It used to be the water tower and may still have the sign. Just after this you meet a road named **Tainters Hill**.

▶ Turn right down the hill and just before the bottom turn left into a road with a very interesting name — **Lower Ladyes Hill**. You will notice the garden areas on your right in front of the row of houses. Further on is a large allotment area - **Oddibourne** allotments.

▶ Continue along passing all the houses in this road until you arrive at a pleasant woodland area - **Kenilworth Common**. This is a nature reserve.

▶ After about 100 yards, take the path on your left by the nature reserve map. The path climbs slightly and then continues through the wooded area towards the north side of the Common. Exit on to **Common Lane**.

▶ Cross over the road and turn right going over the railway bridge and down the hill. Just before the road crosses a stream, you must take a path - like a bridleway- on your right, which goes back into the Common. This path roughly follows the stream and after a short time you will go under a railway arch and pass the old water works buildings which still supply water to Kenilworth.

▶ After a short while look out for a bridge over the stream and cross it into **Forge Road**, named after the smithy which used to be at the far end of the road on the left. Turn right at the end of this road.

▶ After about 20 yards take the path on the right called **The Close**. This takes you past a row of houses facing the Oddibourne allotments on the right. Continue along here to the end and then cross over the road into **School Lane**. (Notice immediately on your left the elaborate **Oddibourne Terrace** with unusual bargeboard porches and fancy brickwork.) Watch out for the path on your right which goes alongside **Finham Brook**. This is a pleasant section of the walk by the side of the brook.

▶ When you reach the road bridge, cross over the brook, go under the bridge and enter Abbey Fields for the last section of your walk.

 ▶ Walk ahead across the park. There are benches and picnic tables if you wish to stop and the toilets are located past the tennis courts and café on your left.

▶ Opposite the café take the path passing the sandstone priory building on your right, and then follow the path round with the lake on the left. The path goes uphill to meet the High Street once again.

▶ Turn left at High Street and follow the road all the way back to the car park keeping the castle in view.

Food and drink are available at the Queen & Castle pub.

Points of Interest:

Founded in the 1120s, **Kenilworth Castle** was built around a powerful Norman great tower and extensively enlarged by King John at the beginning of the 13th century. Local streams were dammed to create water defences and the resulting fortifications withstood assaults throughout 1266. John of Gaunt spent lavishly in the late 14th century, turning the medieval castle into a palace fortress. The Earl of Leicester again extended the castle by constructing new Tudor buildings. In 1649 the castle was partly destroyed by Parliamentary forces. Only two of the buildings remain habitable.

The old hamlet of **Little Virginia** lies close to the castle. Originally consisting of fifteen cottages, which date from the 17th century, it housed the masons and builders employed by Robert Dudley for works on the castle.

St Nicholas' Church has a fine Norman doorway, thought to have been from the earlier St Mary's Abbey. The land on which the church stands is part of a swathe of what, in the 12th century, was the tiny settlement of Chinewerde, given by King Henry I to his Chamberlain and treasurer, Geoffrey de Clinton. By around 1119 this swathe had been cleared of woodland under de Clinton's order so that an Augustinian priory housing 16-20 canons could be built. Geoffrey de Clinton built Kenilworth Castle at around the same time.

Close to St Nicholas' lie the ruins of the **Abbey of St Mary the Virgin**, first founded by Geoffrey de Clinton in 1119 as an Augustine priory. In 1447, the Priory had the unusual distinction of being raised to Abbey status by Henry VI. All that remains now are small parts of the Nave and Chapter House, the gatehouse and another building of unknown origin known today as 'The Barn'.

Parliament Piece, where Henry 111 reputedly held parliament in 1266.

Queen & Castle

Julie M Chiswick

WALK 5: TEMPLE BALSALL
Distance: 4 miles

Parking: Park in Ye Olde Saracen's Head. No charge.

The walk starts from Ye Olde Saracen's Head pub on Balsall Street (B4101) in Balsall Common. It takes in fields and lanes and some road plus interesting buildings in Temple Balsall.

The Walk

OS Explorer map 221 (Coventry and Warwick)

▶ Exit left out of the pub car park and almost immediately left into **Magpie Lane.** Follow the lane and when **Long Brook Lane** joins from the left you continue to the right passing **Magpie Farm** - a black and white timbered building – on your left.

Magpie Farm

▶ Soon afterwards, go left over a hidden stile by a metal gate by a public footpath sign. This section is part of the **Millenium Way.**

▶ Go straight ahead for a short distance and then walk left round the edge of a clump of trees to meet a clear walkway across a field. At the far side you will reach a footbridge and a kissing gate. Go across diagonally left to the next kissing gate.

▶ Continue across the next field on a clearly marked path heading towards a pylon. At the stile go straight across and shortly pass the pylon.

▶ At the next stile, do NOT cross it, but continue straight ahead with the hedge now on your right. **Temple Balsall** can be seen ahead and to the right in the distance. When you reach the road (**Fen End Road**), turn right and soon left into a side road.

▶ Go ahead to meet a wide track, passing the public footpath sign on a metal gatepost. **Poolside Cottage** is to your right. Follow the track round to the right by a farmyard and at the end of the barns turn right. The track then goes left by wooden gates and a stile into a field.

▶ You will notice electricity poles on your left as you walk ahead. At the wooden bridge, you go over a stream and carry on. At the next electricity pole turn 90 degrees right with the hedge on your right.

▶ Continue ahead to the edge of the field where you exit by a wooden kissing gate. You are now in the grounds by the cemetery and to your left a few yards away is a sitting area.

▶ Continue on the gravel path to the next gate and you meet a tarmac path.

▶ Turn right and cross over a wooden bridge. Continue slightly uphill to the **Old Hall** next to the lovely sandstone church of **St Mary's**, Temple Balsall. This is normally open and worth a visit. Close by the church you pass almshouses on your left (they have an interesting history). After the almshouses there is a welcome seat for a drink or snack before the return journey. The school is to your left.

▶ Turn right at the main road, but walk along the tarmac path and go over a long wooden bridge into a car park and out of the metal gates, turning left and back to the main road. (This little diversion avoids a blind bend in the main road).

▶ The next mile is on the road so be aware. It is usually a quiet road, but worth taking care. Turn right at the road and walk for about ¾ mile until you pass **Barracks Cottage** and **Gate Farm** to the left

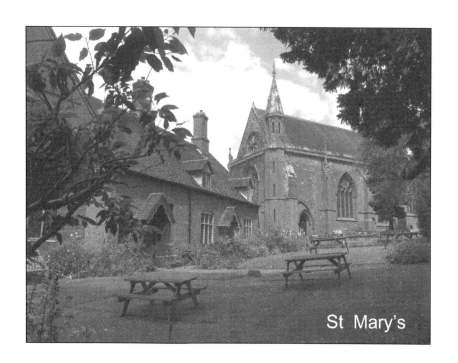

St Mary's

Almshouses

Julie M Chiswick

and **Balsall Lodge** signs followed by **Town Crier Cottage** on the right.

Town Crier Cottage

▶ Continue about ¼ mile and take the first side road on your left which is **Fernhill Lane**. You pass **Brackenford House** on the corner. This is a very peaceful lane to enjoy. At the junction with **Long Brook Lane**, cross ahead keeping on Fernhill Lane.

▶ The road passes over a small, forded stream. In a short while you turn left by **Howlett's Farm** (**Fernhill Cottage** to the right).

▶ After about 20 yards down the driveway, turn right into a field by a waymarker. Follow this field diagonally left towards barns. To the left of the barns is a gap in the hedge by a yellow waymarker.

▶ Go into the next field and continue straight across. You will shortly see houses ahead. As you turn left round a bend at the corner of the field look for a waymarked stile on the right leading into a field close to the houses.

► Go over the stile and cross the last field heading towards the main road (**Balsall Street**).

► Cross one final stile and go along a wooden walkway to the road.

Turn left past the houses and back to the car park at **Ye Olde Saracen's Head**. At the time of writing the pub is open all day.

Ye Olde Saracen's Head

Points of Interest:

Temple Balsall was the headquarters of the Poor Fellow-Soldiers of Christ and of the Temple of Solomon (better known as the Knights Templar).

The rewards for the bravery of the Knights Templar in the Holy Land crusades included gifts of land across Europe. Henry I donated a great complex of estates in England to Roger de Mowbray, a Norman Knight. In an 1185 survey of the Templars' possessions it was noted that Roger de Mowbray was named as the donee of Balsall. The Templars also received gifts of land at Cubbington, Harbury, Tysoe, Wolvey, Studley, Warwick, Chilverscoton, Sherbourne, Fletchampstead, Temple Herdwicke and other places and Temple Balsall became the most important of these. All day-to-day farming activities were controlled from Temple Balsall. Stockbreeding was undertaken and cider apples were brought to the press. The most significant relic of the Templars is their preceptory, now known as the **Old Hall**. This was the senior court for the Templars in Warwickshire. From here instruction and punishment was handed out in equal measure.

The Old Hall

WALK 6: ALVECOTE/ SHUTTINGTON
Distance: 6.0 miles

Parking: At Pooley Country Park. Pay and Display.

The walk starts from the car park at Pooley Country Park. This is reached from Pooley Lane, on the B5000 by Polesworth.

Julie M Chiswick

The Walk

OS Explorer map 232 (Nuneaton and Tamworth)

▶ Walk from the car park, following the path under the motorway bridge. Then cross the canal and turn left onto the towpath at bridge 56. You walk to the right with the canal on your left.

▶ Follow the towpath until bridge 59 (about 15 minutes) where you turn right and follow the road over the railway bridge and through **Alvecote** village. You will pass **Alvecote Cottages** and soon after leaving the village, you will see **Alvecote Meadows Nature Reserve** on your left.

▶ At the end of the road turn right, signposted **Shuttington**. Walk along the footpath about 200 yards and continue over the bridge.

▶ On the far side of the bridge cross the road to a metal gate. Go through the kissing gate and bear slightly right to a small footbridge over a ditch.

▶ Continue uphill across the field to a kissing gate leading into the village of Shuttington. Walk past the houses and village green and this is **Milner Road**. If you need refreshments there is a shop (to your left) and a pub, **The Wolferston Arms**, to your right. It is worth a short detour to visit the small **St Matthew's** church, noted for its fine Norman doorway.

▶ Cross the road into **Church Lane** and the church is just at the end on the highest point of the village.

▶ Retrace your steps back to the field you left earlier. Look across and slightly down the field and in the distance you will see a gate. Cross the field to this gate and then walk onwards to cross a wooden bridge.

▶ Continue in the same direction until you pass a line of trees marking the field boundary on your left. You will also see a large lake on your left which is part of **Alvecote Pools Nature Reserve**. Further on, go through the kissing gate by the metal gate and turn right.

St Matthew's

► Climb two stiles ahead of you and follow the field boundary on your left. Pass through a gate ignoring the stile.

► At the far corner of the field go through two wooden gates into a field with a fence now on your right. Keep following the edge of the field boundary track and continue until you see the track turn to the right and then take a left turn heading towards a row of poplar trees in the distance. At the end of the track cross the stile on your left and follow the concrete road towards the poplars.

► At the edge of the poplars and with the river ahead of you, turn left at the signpost and walk back along the riverside towards a footbridge. Cross this then walk diagonally left before climbing a stile to join a track leading to **Amington**. In Amington, cross the railway and turn slightly left at the T-junction and then straight on to join the towpath at the canal bridge.

► You will enter the towpath at bridge 66. Turn left and follow the path back to Pooley Country Park – about 35 minutes. Approximately halfway you will pass the large marina.

Marina

 There is a café and toilets by the car park and some interesting artifacts and photos from the mining era.

Points of Interest:

The **Anker** flows through the parish of **Shuttington**. Most of the parish is rural although a colliery once existed alongside the railway at Alvecote. A series of pools situated along the river, on the boundary with Tamworth, were created as a result of subsidence caused by mining.

Very little of **Alvecote Priory** survives today and there is no trace of the original building. There was an 18th century house on the site and in its south wall was a 14th-century doorway with moulded jambs and pointed head which probably came from the original Priory. This is all that remains to be seen today.

Amington Hall, a Grade II listed building, is an early 19th century former country house at Amington, now converted into residential apartments.

Amington Hall

WALK 7: HASELEY/GRAND UNION CANAL
Distance: 4 miles

Parking: At The Falcon pub on the A4177 near Haseley. No charge.

A walking stick might be useful in summer in one part where the foliage is a little dense.

The Walk

OS Explorer map 221 (Coventry and Warwick)

▶ Exit the rear of the car park and take the signed grassy path at the side of the field which leads to the church of **St Mary the Virgin**. You will see it almost as soon as you have gone a few yards.

St Mary the Virgin

▶ When you reach the lane by the church turn right and continue to the main road passing **Hatton Village Hall** on the right at the junction.

▶ Go over the road (**A4177**) and continue ahead, passing **The Ferncumbe C of E Primary School** on your left. Follow the path round by the school field and then by the front of houses.

▶ At the next crossroads with the **B4439** keep ahead along a pleasant

Hatton Village Hall

road overhung with trees. As you reach the canal bridge, take the sign-posted towpath on the right, going down steps to meet the canal and continue with the canal on your right. This canal bridge is number 55 (**John's Bridge**).

▶ On this stretch of canal you will see several boats moored and the railway line to your left. After passing **Hatton Station** you will come to bridge 56. Go underneath and up steps on your left to a gate.

▶ Cross over the canal and continue along this lane with houses and bungalows to the left and soon you pass **Oakslade Farm** on the right. Shortly after this, on a right hand bend after a driveway, look for a tricky stile on the left going into a pasture.

▶ You must cross the pasture diagonally, heading slightly left of the large glass roofed building of the garden centre which you will see on the road (B4439).

► Go through the first metal kissing gate and across the next pasture. Exit on to the road through another kissing gate right opposite **Barn Close Nurseries.**

► Cross the road and turn left. Walk about 300 yards and look for a stile on your right at the end of a lay-by. Climb the stile and follow a fenced way which carries on through a wooded area. The walkway can be a bit dense with foliage in the summer.

► Exit the fenced walkway on to the drive of a lovely house named **Shrewley Fields.** Follow the drive and you will pass **The Croft** shortly on your right.

► Climb a corner stile on the left and go through a pasture/paddock towards houses, through a gate, across a small paddock and exit by a stile on to a lane. Cross the lane to a stile into a field.

► Follow the path which soon goes round the right hand side of the field by the hedge until you reach a stile. Turn left on to the unmade lane or vehicle track.

► At the road turn right. Pass the **Little Owl Barn** on the right and about 30 yards after the end of the passing place on your left, look out for a hidden metal gate by an oak tree.

► Go up a few steps, through the gate and straight ahead on a well-defined track through the field towards a house. Keep to the left of the property fence and then exit on to a driveway heading towards the road. You will pass a couple of cottages on the left as you meet the main road.

Cross the road, turn right and head back to The Falcon for a well deserved drink or some food!

Points of Interest:

The **Grand Union Canal** in its current form came into being on 1 January 1929 and was further extended in 1932. It was formed from the amalgamation of several different canals, and at 286.3 miles (461 km) is by far the longest canal in the UK:

London area: Regent's Canal – original company. Hertford Union Canal – bought by the Regent's Canal in 1857.
Main Line: Warwick and Napton Canal – bought by the Regent's Canal in 1927. Warwick and Birmingham Canal – bought by the Regent's Canal in 1927. Birmingham and Warwick Junction Canal – bought by the Regent's Canal in 1927. Grand Junction Canal – bought by the Regent's Canal in 1927
Leicester Line: Old Grand Union Canal – bought by the Grand Junction in 1894. Leicestershire and Northamptonshire Union Canal – bought by the Grand Junction in 1894. Leicester Navigation – bought by the Grand Union in 1932. Loughborough Navigation – bought by the Grand Union in 1932.

Grand Union Canal

WALK 8: HENLEY IN ARDEN
Distance: 5 miles

Parking: There are a couple of free car parks just off High Street (A3400). The one I recommend is the Prince Harry car park. Travel up the High Street from M42 and go left at the traffic lights. Follow the parking signs and they will take you through a residential area to the free car park. There is a walkway through the arch which takes you to the High Street.

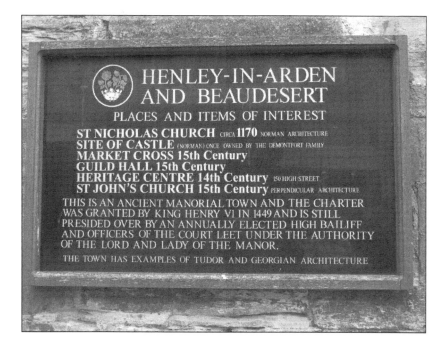

This is a lovely walk but is quite steep at the beginning as you go over The Mount.

The Walk

OS Explorer map 220 (Birmingham south side)

▶ With **St. John's** church on **High Street** on your left, walk down **Beaudesert Lane**, shortly passing a walled garden then the attractive 12th century church of **St Nicholas** on your left. (Worth visiting on the return journey.)

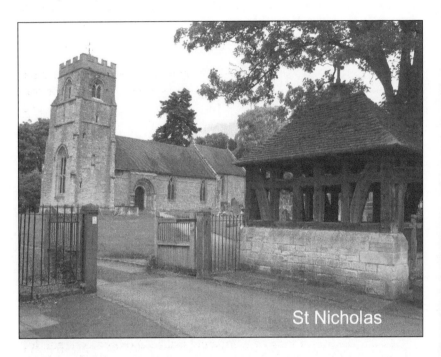
St Nicholas

▶ Continue to a cast iron gate on the left (and a footpath on the right). Go through the gate and climb the steep path to the earthworks which were originally part of the motte and bailey **Beaudesert Castle**. Walk over the crest taking in the views as you go.

▶ Continue on the clear path as it drops down to one of the old defence ditches. There are large, deep wooden steps here down to the ditch. The path continues for a while going up and down and finally

(!) climbing to a wooden bench at the top. Keep ahead and DO NOT take the stile by the bench.

▶ Follow the grassy path ahead and move to the right hand side when you reach the broken fence. After a while and at a waymarker you then turn right through trees to go over a stile.

▶ Cross this field diagonally left to a stile in the far hedge. Turn left on to a track in a woody area. This takes you through trees and after a short distance turn right at a waymarker. This goes across a field with **Hungerfield Farm** soon appearing on your left.

▶ Continue into the next field at the waymarker and follow the clear path round the edge of the field with the hedge on your left. At the corner of the hedge, go straight across the field to a metal kissing gate and through a tiny copse.

▶ Cross another field to a kissing gate and follow a track slightly uphill and over the brow you will see **Holly Bank Farm** in the dip to your left.

▶ Go through another kissing gate and cross this next field diagonally where you go through a gap in the hedge and join the road ahead **(Henley Road)**. As you exit through the farm gates on to the road, turn left and walk about 450 yards.

▶ At the bend, turn right into the northern end of **Preston Field Lane** (an unmade lane). You will immediately pass a house called **Willow-brook Barn** on your left and then continue down the lane. Soon you
(!) will pass over a ford by a concrete bridge and then continue for about 750 yards up this lane with trees on either side. It could be muddy here if there has been a lot of rain.

▶ When you reach a tarmac lane by **Lilac Cottage**, go ahead. This is
(←) **Rookery Lane** and has some interesting houses to look at. At a small triangle of grass with a willow tree, keep right and continue until you reach **Preston Bagot** church (**All Saints**), tucked off the lane to your right. It is signposted and you enter the churchyard by a wooden gate. There are benches by the church if you wish to have a

coffee or snack.

All Saints

▶ Follow the footpath (church on your right) out to the left by the gate and straight ahead to a wooden kissing gate. The path soon becomes enclosed by hedges and goes steeply downhill. You will pass **The Old Rectory** on your right and then reach a road. (At the time of writing there is an art barn in the grounds of the rectory which is worth a visit.)

▶ At the road, go straight across and through the gate opposite. The next part crosses several fields keeping on the public footpath. Firstly, go across two small fields with kissing gates and a barn to your right. Then cross the next larger field keeping the hedge on the right until you reach the kissing gate. In the next field go across the centre to a further kissing gate.

① ▶ Continue immediately through yet another kissing gate bearing right with the hedge on your right. Leave this field at a kissing gate into an orchard belonging to **Barn View**. You should now have reached part of **Edge Lane**.

▶ Turn left to soon pass **Kyte Green Farm** and then a cottage. Keep ahead on Edge Lane and on a right hand bend you will pass a farm off to the left and then a lovely house and farm with barns on your right.

Ⓘ Keep going and follow about 6 electricity poles until you find an old stile partially hidden on the right. (If you reach the engineering building on the right, you have gone too far.)

▶ Go over the stile and walk across the field with the hedge on the right. At the end, go over the stile on the right and then find steps and a stile into a large wooded area. The steps are wide and go steeply downhill through the woods to a grassy play area.

▶ Over to the right you will see a gated walkway. Take this and you will exit on **Castle Close**. Go straight across to continue on the walkway passing the school on your left. Carry on along the edge of the school grounds and turn left at the end of the school fence to follow round the perimeter.

▶ The narrow path continues with trees on the left and **The Mount** to your right. Exit on **Meadow Road** and in the corner by a house, the walkway continues, skirting the side of the house. It finally emerges on **Beaudesert Lane** once more and you are back to the start of your walk.

🍸☕ For refreshments there are the **White Swan** opposite Beaudesert Lane, the **Bluebell** off to the right or the wonderful **Henley Ice Cream Shop** to the left as you make your way back to the car park.

If you have time, **High Street** has some interesting buildings, so worth having a look.

🍸 If you wish to travel a little further, the **Crab Mill** in **Preston Bagot** is excellent for food and ambience.

Points of Interest:

The one mile long **High Street** is a conservation area and contains over 150 buildings listed as being of Special Architectural or Historic Interest. Notable among them is the **Guild Hall**, a timber-framed building standing to the north of **St. John's Church**. It has been extensively restored though many of the original timbers remain. The Guild Hall is where the Court Leet, an ancient manorial court, meets every November to elect its officers and report on the work of the year.

In the centre of the town is the old **Market Place**, where stands the remains of the 15th century **Market Cross**, one of the few still existing in Warwickshire. The Cross is built of local stone, but only the raised base of three steps and the lower part of the shaft remain. Originally the cross had a four-sided head with niches, each with a carved relief: the Rood, the Trinity, St. Peter with the key and possibly the Virgin and Child. Proclamations have been made from the Cross for more than five centuries, including the proclamation of the accession of Queen Elizabeth II in 1952.

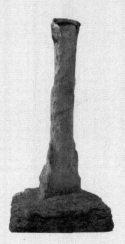

Joseph Hardy House, home of the Heritage Centre, is itself a rare architectural gem. The oldest parts of the house have been dated to 1345.

WALK 9: HARTSHILL
Distance: 4 miles

The Anchor Inn is on the B4111, between Atherstone and Nuneaton. Park in the pub car park. No charge.

The walk takes in the Coventry canal, part of Hartshill Country Park , Hartshill Green and a quiet lane at the end. It is a great walk for summer days as there are no fields of crops to cross.

The Walk

OS Explorer map 232 (Coventry and Nuneaton)

►Exit the car park of the **Anchor Inn** and walk across the front of the pub to enter the canal towpath at bridge 29. .

►Go under this and continue under bridge 30. Before the next bridge is a mooring area on the left and a cosmetic factory masked by trees to the right.

The Anchor Inn

►Continue under bridge 31 by the waterways maintenance depot – an interesting listed building – on the left and then almost immediately go under bridge 32.

►Continue for a short time and leave the towpath at bridge 33. Go up

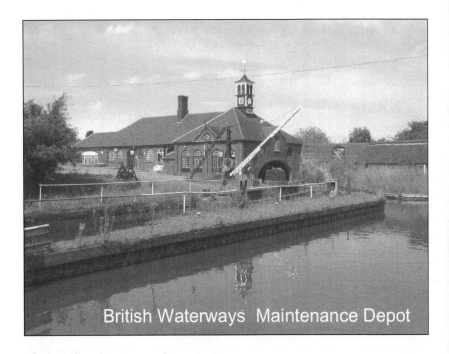

British Waterways Maintenance Depot

steps to a metal gate and over the canal through another gate –well sign-posted.

►Walk over the field on a clear track towards houses, passing an electricity pole on the right.

►At the end of the field, turn right on a vehicle track. Do not go straight ahead up the steps! Keep on the track even though you will pass a right hand track to **Cherry Tree Farm**.

►Keep going for a while and you will go through some shade along this track until you reach a 5 bar gate and a kissing gate. Go through this and continue left along the rough field with the woods on your left.

►Continue for quite a while along the edge of the woods until you come to an old gate by a wooden stile.

►Continue straight ahead keeping **outside** the woods and you will be climbing uphill towards the top of **Hartshill Country Park**. Ignore any gates or paths to your left until you arrive at a wooden kissing gate in the corner. Go through this and you are in the area with some benches and picnic tables further over.

►Turn left on the path with the woods on your left and continue a short distance to the car park, then left to the café and toilets. You will also pass a children's play area.

►With the toilets on your left, take the path through a metal gate. In about 100 yards the path divides. You must go right. Soon after this the path divides again and you take the left path going steeply downhill. This continues for a while through the woodland walk. The track is quite obvious as you walk down to the bottom.

►In the valley and by a wide vehicle track, turn left and then almost immediately right by a waymarker and a triangular stone seat sculpture. Keep descending a good distance until you go over a tree trunk foot-bridge over a small stream.

►Continue ahead going uphill and down, passing another waymarker on the right and then after a fair distance you will arrive at a narrow stone walkway.

►Continue along this walkway and up several wide steps on the other side. (There is a bench part way up if you feel like a rest.) At the top exit through a large metal gate on to a road.

►Turn right and walk along to **Hartshill Green**. Cross the road at **The Green** and go in front of the **Stag and Pheasant** pub walking to the right.

►Take the first lane on the left which is **Grange Road**. Along here you will pass the **Malt Shovel** pub and **Hartshill Methodist Chapel** on your left.

►At the end of the houses the lane narrows and you pass playing fields on the left. The lane starts to go downhill, but look out for the interesting sculpture and explanation board. The sculpture has three sides and shows jobs and industry around the area and

Hartshill Methodist Chapel

also one side is dedicated to Michael Drayton, a Warwickshire poet born in Hartshill in 1563.

►Continue steeply downhill passing a junction on the left with a 'weak bridge' sign. Do not turn here, but continue downhill passing an old black and white Grade 11 listed building on the right called **Hartshill Grange**.

►Continue to canal bridge (30) and turn right to go on to the towpath and then walk left with the canal on your right.

►Exit at the next bridge (29) to the Anchor Inn. You can walk through the canal side garden to return to the car park.

 Refreshments can be had at the Anchor Inn, the Stag and Pheasant and the Malt Shovel.

Points of Interest:

British Waterways Maintenance Depot on Coventry Canal. This Grade II listed building, a covered dock and workshops, dates to the mid 19th century.

Hartshill Methodist Chapel. Closed in 2012 after 175 years of worship owing to a declining congregation.

Hartshill Sculpture depicts a history of local people and trades, including Michael Drayton, a Hartshill poet who came to prominence in the Elizabethan era.

Hartshill Grange, a Grade II listed building dating from the early 16th century.

Hartshill Sculpture

WALK 10: KNOWLE LOCKS
Distance: 4.5 miles

The Kings Arms is on the A4141 to the south of Knowle. Park in the pub car park. No charge.

This walk passes the interesting Knowle Locks twice – going up the flight and coming down. It goes along quiet lanes with a short section through fields and a walk through an attractive residential area.

The Walk

OS Explorer map 220 (Birmingham, south side)

The **King's Arms** used to be the Heron's Nest. Prior to that it was, in fact, the King's Arms and after a delightful refurbishment in 2014, it has its original name once more.

The King's Arms

▶ Exit the car park and pass in front of the pub to pick up the towpath on the right at bridge 70. Turn right under the bridge with the canal now on your left.

▶ After about ½ mile you will see the beginning of **Knowle Locks** - a flight of five locks. In the distance on the left standing on a small hill is a large newly extended house known as **Batts Hall**.

Knowle Locks looking north

Knowle Locks looking south

► As you get to the last lock you will pass **Top Lock View** – a house on the right hand side of the path. Further on you will see the boat-building company at **Knowle Hall Wharf** and you must exit the towpath here at bridge 71. You are now on the B4101 (**Kenilworth Road**).

Knowle Hall Wharf

► Turn right here for a short distance to **Elvers Green Lane** on your left. Keep ahead down this quiet lane passing a few houses on your right and then **Elvers Green Farm**.

► Continue for a short while. On a sharp right hand bend you will pass a private drive on the left. Go past this and soon after on your left take a stile by a metal gate.

► Follow the path round the edge of a field with a wooden fence firstly on the left, then a small copse. Then the hedge continues on your left. Look out soon for a public footpath going left by a wooden gate in the hedge.

▶ Continue along with a field fence on your left and a house behind the hedge on your right.

▶ At the end of the field fence, cross over the tarmac drive (leading to **Torwood House**) and go over the stile opposite. This takes you by a large copse known as **Nappins Covert**.

▶ Keep ahead through a gate with a yellow public footpath sign. At the end of the copse by a very close pylon, cross the stile you see and walk right with the hedge now on your right.

▶ Follow this edge of the field and it soon becomes a vehicle track. Keep ahead all the way on this track. Exit the track by a double wooden gate at the side of **Waterfield Farm**.

▶ Go left to meet the main road. Turn left at the road and enter the canal towpath on your left after about 100 yards. This is bridge 73 and you walk left along the towpath with the canal now on your right.

▶ Go under the footbridge 72A and continue to bridge 72 where you leave the canal.

▶ Turn left back over the bridge and follow the small lane (**Kixley Lane**) passing 'The Cottage' on your right and a couple of houses. Soon you will pass more houses both to the right and the left. At the main road (B4101) turn left.

▶ Walk along this pleasant residential area of large houses and when you see the Knowle Hall Wharf sign, the towpath is just over the bridge on your right. Continue back on the towpath going past the locks again (which look very different looking down the locks). You will exit the towpath at bridge 70 opposite the garden of the King's Arms pub.

 Enjoy refreshments at the King's Arms, or in Knowle where there are many pubs and cafés.

WALK 11: ULLENHALL
Distance: 4.5 miles

The Winged Spur is on Ullenhall Lane in the centre of the village. Park in the pub car park. No charge.

This pretty walk is very rural. Ullenhall is a small village and I have tried to include a church, a chapel, fields and lanes, a portion of the Arden Way and some public footpaths.

The Walk

OS Explorer map 220 (Birmingham, south side)

▶ The walk starts from the pub car park turning left towards the war memorial just in front of a building known as **The Old Central Stores**.

The Memorial

▶ Turn down the lane to the left of this building and at a T-junction go left with **The Brook House** on your right. The small brook runs on your left. This is **Watery Lane**.

▶ Continue down this lane and turn right by houses at **Perry Mill Lane**. A little further on you pass a bungalow called **Greenlands** on your left and after a short distance go up a few steps to a gate on your left.

▶ Follow ahead through the field to a wooden gate and a metal kissing gate on the opposite side.

▶ Cross **Tanworth Road** and go straight ahead along a lane signposted to **Blunt's Green**. As the road bends to the left, you go right to follow the **Arden Way**. There is a sign for a dead end.

▶ At the end of this short lane is **Old Chapel Cottage** on the right and just ahead is the **Old Chapel** (worth a look) set in lovely grounds. You leave Arden Way here and retrace steps to a gate opposite the cottage and take the public footpath across the field with four oak trees to your right. On the far side of the field, close to a house, you exit on to a lane.

Old Chapel

▶ Go ahead and immediately on the right, take a metal gate in the hedge to follow the public footpath bearing right.

▶ After a very short distance, go through a kissing gate on the right into a field.

Julie M Chiswick

▶ Head towards a marker and stile almost in the centre of the wooden post and rail fence. This has been put in by the farmer.

▶ Go over a high wooden stile and head across the field to the left of the oak tree, towards a gate. You will see stable buildings to the left. Exit by the metal gate and after a few yards you meet a lane.

▶ Take the metal gate almost opposite (not the 5 bar gate). Go across a small field to another metal gate (passing farm buildings on the right).

▶ Continue diagonally right across this large field going slightly uphill. You will not see the next marker until at the brow of the hill. The gate is in the top right hand corner of the field by a fence.

▶ Cross over to another gate and continue on a well-marked grassy path going downhill towards a red-roofed house.

▶ At the bottom of the grassy path, to the right of the house, you exit by a metal gate by a marker and follow a narrow track round and between houses to meet a lane.

▶ Turn right at the lane passing **The Croft** on your right and then **College Farm** drive also on the right. Continue along the lane.

▶ Soon after **12 Elms House** the Arden Way joins the lane from the right. Continue ahead towards the tiny hamlet of **Hallsend**. When you reach **The Cottage** and **Little Hall**, take a bridleway which goes between these two houses.

▶ Go over two stiles and onto the bridleway (which could be damp as it's overhung by trees).

▶ Go over a rickety stile by a gate and continue a very short distance. Before the next gate, you must turn to the right and go over an old wooden stile into a field. Turn left, keeping the hedge on your left, and head towards the house tucked down in the trees.

▶ As you get to the corner, you will see a pond on the left. Turn round the edge of the field and soon exit on to a lane right by **Hall End Farm**. The correct path stays along the field edge, but I spoke with the very kind farmer and he said it was fine to walk along his farm track instead.

▶ Turn right at the farm and follow the farm track, which soon changes into a lane. Shortly after this you will see double metal gates on the left close to a well-hidden kissing gate with an Arden Way marker.

▶ Go straight across with the hedge on your left going slightly uphill. The field is rather uneven. By a large tree partway up the field you will see a kissing gate and markers.

▶ Continue through and into the next field to the Old Chapel at the end in the trees.

▶ Go through the graveyard and out onto the lane which you may recognise from earlier.

▶ At the next road go left and continue to the road. Go straight across through a metal gate and into the field. Continue straight across and exit by a gate and down steps to the lane.

▶ Cross the lane to another metal gate and continue into the last field with the hedge on your left. At the far end of the field bear right, keeping to the edge of a house fence. The path is easy to see from here and goes by the side of the house to the next lane.

▶ At the junction go right and up to the memorial where you started the walk. The pub is just on the right after this.

▶ Opposite the pub is a narrow alleyway between houses. Take this and it brings you into a pasture. Walk across and the church is on the far side. Retrace your steps to return to The Winged Spur where refreshments can be had.

NOTE: If you wish to see the parish church – **St Mary the Virgin** – it is a very short deviation from the pub.

(At the time of writing the church was not open to the public for viewing purposes.)

The Winged Spur

Points of Interest:

In 1808 John Booth, son of John Booth of Hall End Farm, was found in a stable with severe head wounds. Was he killed by a 'vicious mare' or by his brother, William, who was visiting the farm? William was tried for the murder and was acquitted. However, William was also a forger. He converted the top floor of the farmhouse into a workshop where he produced forgeries of coins and banknotes.

He was caught and sentenced to hang, but his execution was bungled, and he fell through the scaffold's trap door to the floor. He was hanged again and died.

William Booth was probably the last person to be sentenced to death in England for forgery.

Hall End Farm

WALK 12: BAXTERLEY
Distance: 5.5 miles

The Rose lies at the centre of the hamlet of Baxterley. It can be reached from the A5 via Baddesley Ensor or the B4116 from Coleshill. Park in the pub car park. No charge.

The walk takes in agricultural scenery, fields, farms, lanes and some quiet road walking at the end. In summer the crops and foliage can be quite high, so it may be better as a spring or autumn walk after a dry period of weather. A walking stick would be helpful if you do choose to go in summer.

The Walk

OS Explorer map 232 (Nuneaton and Tamworth)

▶ Leave the car park with **The Rose** on your left. Go straight ahead and this is a continuation of **Main Road**. You pass houses on your left, a park area on the right and then more houses on the right.

The Rose

▶ Go round the bend after the houses and after the next bend, take a driveway on your left leading down to **Kiddles Farm**. Go through the farmyard and continue on a track past the farmhouse and into a field. Follow the track and at the end of it go into another field ahead with the hedgerow on your right. Keep to the edge.

▶ Follow the hedgerow round to the right and then go left on to a wide track of soft wood chippings. This is a gallop track for horses kept in the area and is used mainly from March to September. You will soon walk past a low hedgerow on the right. (To your left on the other side of the field is **Drybrooks Wood**. At the end of the wood you can see **Boultbees Farm**.) Keep on the gallop track passing a line of eight trees on the left.

▶ Continue all the way to the end of the track to the trees at the far end. In the trees is a hidden wooden bridge going across a small stream. Go across it and left through the copse (a stick might be handy if overgrown). Exit into a field close to the road.

▶ Go round the edge of the field to the right with the tree line on your right and you will meet the road (**Atherstone Lane**). Continue to the right heading towards the outskirts of **Hurley**. The lane goes gently up-hill and then flattens out and you will soon pass **Hurley Hall Farm** on your left.

Carry on past the farm and look out for the moat in the grounds of the hall.

Hurley Hall Farm

▶ Continue ahead and follow the road round a sharp right hand bend signposted Hurley and you will see **Hurley Lane** on your left and some houses on the left.

▶ At the next sharp bend you take the road right signposted 'Baxterley and Atherstone'. This is **Heanley Lane** – a quiet country lane.

▶ You pass the small wooden 'missionary' church on your left (**Church of the Resurrection**), followed by **School House** and **Hurley Primary School**. Then an unusual black and white cottage on the right.

▶ Further along the lane is a small cemetery on the right. Continue a little further and after a metal gate (on the left) count two electricity poles on your right and you should find a hidden metal kissing gate on the right by the second pole. (Again the walking stick may be useful in the summer months.)

▶ Go left round the edge of the field (even if it has crops close by) and part way down the long side of the field look out for a metal kissing gate in the hedge. You should see **Cottage Farm** ahead of you before you reach the kissing gate.

▶ Go through the gate into the next field, once more keeping the hedge on your left. Continue round the edge of the field (may also have crops) and continue until you reach a metal gate in a corner – easier to see this time.

▶ Go through the gate and turn right down a narrow track between hedges towards **Hipsley Farm Cottages**. Turn left at the lane and follow it round passing farm holiday cottages and **Hipsley Paddock**.

▶ Keep along this lane and you will come to a large bungalow and grounds on the left called **Moat Close**. Continue round the left hand bend to pass **Latimer's Cottages** and **Latimer's Place** (named after Bishop Hugh Latimer). Just after this turn left down a driveway to visit **Baxterley Church**.

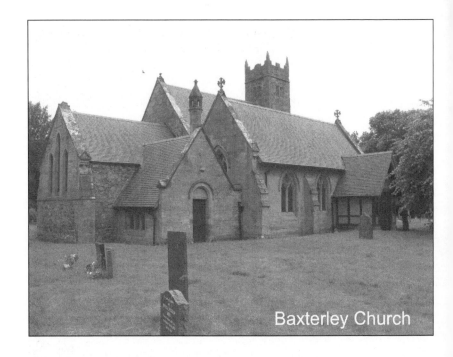

Baxterley Church

▶ Retrace steps back to the road and go ahead to complete the last part of the walk on the road passing various farms as you go. You are now on Main Road heading back to Baxterley. This stretch is approximately 1½ miles. On the way look out for several places – firstly **Pump House Farm** and then **White's Farm** which is an equestrian centre with livery stables. On a bend in the road you will pass **Rose Farm** on the left and **Charity Farm** to the right.

▶ Soon after on the left is a track to **Baxterley Hall Farm.** This was probably originally in the grounds of the old manor house, **Baxterley Hall.** Only the gatehouse remains, almost directly opposite the Rose Inn.

After this you are back to the houses of Baxterley village and a short walk back to The Rose car park.

 The Rose is a popular pub that serves good traditional food.

Points of Interest:

The Rose Inn overlooks the village green and duck pond. Originally believed to be a 'Gentleman's residence', it dates back to the 18th century. Before serving the public it functioned as a courthouse, jail and mortuary.

Baxterley Hall gatehouse (directly opposite The Rose and currently lived in) is the remaining trace of a substantial manor house. Baxterley Hall, built in 1548, was demolished in 1849.

The Church of the Resurrection was built in 1861 of wood with a cast iron frame, originally as a school. It was also used for Sunday services. The school later moved to a purpose built brick building not far from this structure. That was demolished in 1998, replaced by the present school. The foundations of the old school are still visible in the car park.

Church of The Resurrection

WALK 13: LAPWORTH LOCKS AND PACKWOOD
Distance: 4.5 miles

The Boot is situated on the B4439 in Lapworth.. Park in the pub car park. No charge.

This walk goes along the Lapworth flight of locks, across several fields with picturesque views, passes Lapworth Church, Packwood House and the Packwood Avenue walkway returning along country roads and back on to the canal for a few minutes.

The Walk

OS Explorer map 220 (Birmingham south side)

▶ From the rear of **The Boot** car park take the entrance on to the canal towpath and turn left with the beginning of the flight on your left. The first one you see is lock 14. Follow the path along to **Lock Cottage** at bridge 32 where you cross over to the other side.

Lock Cottage, Bridge 32

▶ Continue along the towpath, under bridge 31 and on to bridge 30. Just past here on the left take the footpath sign through a wooden gate right by the side of **Lapworth Cricket Club**.

▶ Go across this rough pasture heading diagonally right to the corner of the field. Then keeping the tree line on your right you head towards the marker and a stile. Go through the gap by the stile and straight across the next field towards trees. There is also a stream running through the trees on the left.

▶ At the bottom of the field, go through a metal kissing gate into a copse. With a pond on your left, continue on a grassy track to the next kissing gate by a yellow marker. Continue on the grassy path towards a 5 bar gate and stile to a lane.

▶ Head straight across to a walkway (cemetery on the left) and continue a short distance to **St Mary the Virgin**. As you leave the church you must cross the road and go straight across to a field going downhill and with stables on your left.

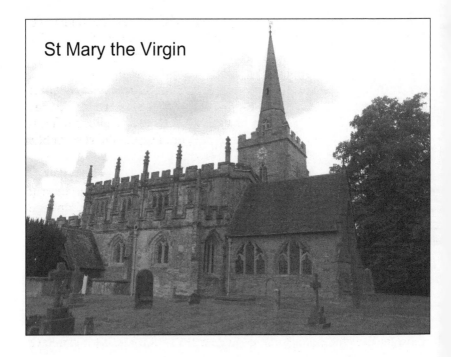
St Mary the Virgin

▶ Go over a stile and continue ahead up and down to trees and a kissing gate at the bottom.

▶ Go through and over a small wooden bridge to other side. Then turn 90 degrees right and head towards the next marker by a 5 bar gate. Continue ahead through a field with a barbed wire fence to the left.

▶ At the next stile (Millennium Way marker) go up the field straight ahead with a large tree just at the top by the stile. Go over this stile, through the next field and exit into the farmyard of **Drawbridge Farm**. At the end of the farmyard, go over the canal drawbridge and walk to a lane ahead.

▶ Turn left, walk about 50 yards and cross the road to pick up a public footpath by a large metal gate. Go straight ahead through this long field towards a gap in the tree line.

▶ After the gap go right, keeping close to the tree line on your right. In the far corner, hidden away, is your next stile. Go over this and follow a grassy walkway to the driveway of a large gated property.

▶ Turn right and walk down the drive with Victorian streetlights. Meet **Grove Lane** at the end and go straight across to pick up a public footpath in the grounds of **Packwood House**, a National Trust property. Do not head for the lake, but keep to the clear public footpath marker posts ahead of you.

▶ The posts take you round the edge of the grounds and you exit shortly to the right by a metal kissing gate into another field. Continue round the left hand edge by the trees until you reach a metal gate and wooden walkway.

▶ Keep following the track with the edge of the wood on your left and a wooden fence by a large garden on your right. Exit on to **Packwood Lane**. Turn left here and follow the lane about ¼ mile towards Packwood House. It can be a busy lane especially at weekends! You will soon see the house and gardens on your left – worth a visit if you have time.

▶ If you are continuing the walk without stopping at Packwood, turn right just as you go through the brick gateposts. Follow the grass track to semi circular stone steps with a metal gate. You are now going to follow a wide grass, tree-lined track known as **The Avenue**. This continues for about ¾ mile and you exit on to **Chessett's Wood Road**.

▶ Turn right and continue along here passing some extremely large houses – **Chessett's House**, **Lightwoods** and **Broadoaks** on the right and **Baddersley Holt** on the left. After almost ½ mile you reach a cross-roads.

▶ Go straight across with **The Punchbowl** on your right. This is a very pleasant eatery at the time of writing. You are now in **Mill Lane**. Continue along for about ½ mile until you pass over a canal bridge by some houses.

▶ As you cross the bridge (34), drop down immediately to the tow-path on your right.

▶ Turn left with the canal on your right, and within a few minutes you will arrive at The Boot where refreshments can be had.

The Boot Inn

Points of Interest:

St Mary the Virgin, a grade 1 listed building, dates from around 1100 AD. A stone church existed on the site of the present nave and chancel. Building work began in the 12th century and continued for the next 300 years.

Lapworth Locks
The locks which make up Lapworth flight on the Stratford-upon-Avon Canal are reckoned to be some of the most interesting to be found on English canals. They are very narrow, permitting the passage of a single narrowboat only. There are some other interesting features along this stretch of the canal, one of which is a drawbridge close by Drawbridge Farm.

Packwood House is a beautiful, timber-framed Tudor house with additional building in the 17th century. The house is the centrepiece of a formal Carolean garden and a yew garden representing the Sermon on the Mount.

Lapworth Locks

WALK 14: WOOTTON WAWEN
Distance: 4 miles

The Navigation Inn is situated on the A3400 to the south-east of the village. Park in the pub car park. No charge.

This walk takes in part of the Stratford-on-Avon canal close to an aqueduct, passes Yew Tree Farm Craft Centre and follows The Monarch's Way heading to Austy Woods. Then through fields, crossing the river Alne and to the Saxon Sanctuary (Warwickshire's oldest church.) Finish by visiting Wootton Hall and its residential village before returning to the Navigation Inn.

The Walk

OS Explorer map 220 (Birmingham south side)

▶ Go along the back of the pub towards the **Anglo-Welsh Narrow-boats** moorings. Once at the canal, look to the left and you will see the aqueduct. Constructed in 1813, it is unusual in the fact that the walkway adjacent to the aqueduct is below the level of the canal. Retrace steps to the car park and turn right at the road to start the walk.

Anglo-Welsh's narrowboats

▶ Go in front of the **Navigation Inn,** under the aqueduct and right into **Pettiford Lane** with **Yew Tree Farm Craft Centre** on your left. You may wish to stop for a visit on your return journey.

▶ Just after the craft centre take a lane on the right by a house named **Apple Trees**. This takes you to the canal bridge 53. Turn left before

Aqueduct, Stratford-upon-Avon Canal

the bridge to pick up the towpath with the canal on your right.

▶ You will soon pass by a little bridge 52, and then carry on for a few hundred yards to bridge 51, **Green Lane Bridge**. Go over this bridge and meander through a tree-lined track which is part of **The Monarch's Way**.

▶ Continue on this with fields to your right. You will then come to **Austy Woods**. Keep following this track which goes along the edge of the woods, getting wider for a while. As the wood becomes less dense the track narrows again and starts to rise. Be aware that the path could be muddy in parts after a lot of rain.

▶ When you are on the flat again keep your eyes open for a track off to the right. It may have a sign saying **Private Land**, but I have been assured by a local farmer that it is perfectly fine to take this track which heads through the centre of the wood. This is a popular bluebell walk in the springtime and was a bridleway. After about

¾ mile you will exit on to the main road by steps past a small brick building.

▶ Turn right for a short distance until you reach the driveway of **Austy Manor**. Cross the road here to a metal gate leading into a field. Go diagonally right across this field to a stile in the hedge with a marker.

▶ Head across the next rather rough field in a similar direction, keeping white cottages in your sights in the distance. As you reach the other side of the field you will be able to see canal bridge 54. Go over this bridge and down a lane passing a couple of bungalows on the right.

▶ Turn left at the lane **(Pennyford Lane)**, passing by **Field Farm**. Immediately after this go through the metal gate on your right. Go straight across with the farm and then stables on your right and follow a narrow path in between wooden poles and the hedge. The poles may possibly have netting stretched across them.

▶ Exit this narrow path by a wooden gate and go ahead through the next field. Veer right to the next gate passing a bit of a scrappy area at the back of the farm! Keep in the same direction and look out for steps and a hidden footbridge in the trees. Go across the footbridge over the **River Alne**.

▶ As you leave the footbridge look right to see the church in the distance. Follow the grassy path in this direction. After a short distance you will exit the grassy path by a metal kissing gate by a cottage.

▶ Walk across to a wooden 5 bar gate and go ahead towards the main road. Cross the road to visit **St Peter's** church, known as the **Saxon Sanctuary**. It is the oldest church in Warwickshire and well worth a visit.

▶ Retrace steps to the road and turn left into the grounds of **Wootton Hall**. You can walk down the drive to see the hall (from the outside) and if you wish you can take a short walk past the post box and round the 'residential village', but you will have to retrace steps to the road once again for the final section of the walk.

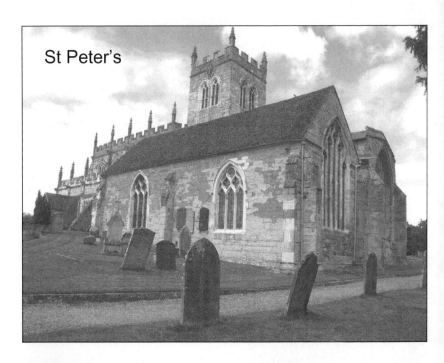

St Peter's

Weir on the River Alne

▶ Turn left at the road (**A3400**) and continue for about 100 yards where you will cross the River Alne and have a good view of the weir. Shortly after this is the old mill conversion – now flats and apartments. A few yards on is the little cemetery belonging to the Catholic church and then you are back at Pettiford Lane should you wish to visit the farm shop and craft centre.

 ▶ Otherwise continue a few more yards to the car park at the Navigation Inn where you can obtain refreshments. Or visit the **Bull's Head** in Wootton Wawen village.

The Navigation Inn

Points of Interest:

Saint Peter's is the oldest church in Warwickshire, notable for its pronounced Anglo-Saxon work. It contains a small library of 17th-century theological works together with some notable monumental brasses.

The aqueduct, constructed in 1813, that carries the Stratford-upon-Avon Canal over the A3400.

The timber-framed **Bull's Head**, thought to date from the 16th century. However, there is a stone inside claiming the date of the building as 1317.

Wootton Hall, a stone building in the Palladian style, mainly built in 1687 but incorporating parts of an earlier, probably Elizabethan, house. It was originally the home of the Carington family. Since 1958 it has served as the headquarters of Allen's Caravans. Outbuildings behind the house may be the remains of an earlier manor house.

Wootton Hall

WALK 15: HAWKESBURY JCT.
Distance: 5 miles

Parking: There are parking spaces on the left as you enter Hawkesbury Junction , by Bridge 11 and before you reach The Greyhound.

The walk touches the Coventry and Oxford canals, gentle countryside and fishing lakes. You will see a fine example of a Victorian cast iron bridge at Hawkesbury Junction and possibly some interesting wildlife in this conservation area. There is a lot to see at Hawkesbury Junction where many narrowboats are moored. The junction is also known as Sutton Stop.

Julie M Chiswick

The Walk

OS Explorer map 221 (Coventry and Warwick)

▶ Start the walk from the car park by bridge 11. Turn right along the towpath passing under an interesting bridge (11A) with metal bird and fish sculptures attached

Bridge 11A

▶ Cross over the cast iron footbridge with the **Greyhound Inn** to your right and a canal fork ahead. Take the right fork. Cross the footbridge over the **Oxford Canal** and then go left along the towpath with the canal on your left.

▶ As the towpath bends right you pass by very obvious electricity pylons and lines. Continue to reach bridge 4 **(Tusses Bridge)**. At the side of a large house you must ascend to the **Coventry Road** (B4019). (This house is on the site of the old Elephant and Castle.)

The Greyhound

▶ On Coventry Road turn left, crossing the bridge over the canal and follow the road for a short distance past houses on the right, until you see **The Old Crown** public house on the corner of **Lentons Lane**. You will then pass the entrance to the National Grid on the left and several more houses including the quaint **Hawkesbury Lodge** – the last house on the left. In a few yards, just before a large sign for 'Nuneaton and Bedworth', take a public footpath to the right down the side of **Parrott's Grove**. This is a grassy track which goes through bushes and trees and later between hedges.

▶ Exit by a stile into a large field. Go diagonally right across the field, heading towards a farm in the far left corner. This is **Sowe Fields Farm**. In the corner is a metal 5 bar gate and a high stile. Go over this into another field.

▶ Head straight across the field towards trees on the far side and after a few yards you will be able to see the stile by the trees. Continue across

Julie M Chiswick   85

to the next stile ahead – marked FOOTPATH.

▶ Go over the next high stile! Continue along the right hand edge by the hedgerow. You will clearly see **Trossachs Farm** to your left.

▶ Go next through a metal 5 bar gate (no stile) and then another 5 bar gate to a farm drive. Cross the farm drive to another 5 bar gate and go through into a small fenced paddock area. (At the time of writing there were a few horses on the other side of the fence.)

▶ At the end of this, turn right towards a stile and a small wooden plank over a streamlet.

▶ Go diagonally right over the next large field heading to the left of a solitary ash tree. (If the field is ploughed, you will be able to walk to the right going round the edge to get to the tree.) About 20 yards to the left of the ash tree is a gate and this leads on to the **Coventry Way**.

▶ Turn left after the gate on to the track and follow it for a short while as it bends round the edge of a field heading to the Coventry Road. You will pass close by **Mile Tree Farm**. At the end of the field exit to the road by a stile tucked in the left corner.

▶ Cross the road to the signs for **Hollyhurst Lakes** – two lakes stocked for fishing. Continue ahead on a track past the lakes in the direction of **Hollyhurst Farm**. Keep left on the Coventry Way when the path forks. There is a waymarker post a bit further up and you must go through a gap in the hedge.

▶ Follow this narrow track passing by a house and then a barn on the left. A few yards on go through a kissing gate into a small copse. Exit close to another kissing gate on to a grass track. This area is a nature reserve called **Coalpit Field Woodlands**. Go left on the track as shown by the marker.

▶ After passing under some electricity lines you will see a stile on your left to a farm track. Go over this and turn right up this track. Veer left at the end to head towards the canal again. As you approach the canal bridge no 13, you may notice some stables and horses to your right.

▶ Just before the bridge, go left and descend to the towpath. Head left with canal on your right. This is now the **Coventry Canal** and part of the **Centenary Way.** This last stretch of the walk is approximately ¾ mile before you reach **Hawkesbury Junction.**

 The Greyhound Inn, voted the best pub in Coventry 4 times, is a traditional canalside venue dating from the early 1800s.

 Adjoining the pub, the cottages at 4-14 Sutton Stop are listed Grade II buildings. It is thought that these were originally associated with the old Victoria Colliery which lay on land to the rear.

Coventry Canal

Points of Interest:

Hawkesbury Junction is located at the northern limit of the Oxford Canal where it meets the Coventry Canal. The junction is also known locally as **Sutton Stop,** after the Sutton family who were well known lock-keepers for more than half of the nineteenth century. Hawkesbury has long been an iconic place in canal folklore, particularly during the days of coal boats waiting for orders at the toll office.

Britannia Bridge. Cast at the Britannia Foundry in Derby, this structure has a span of 50 feet. The abutments are constructed in red handmade bricks with a semicircular blue brick coping.

The Engine House once housed a Newcomen type engine which had already seen around one hundred years' service at one of the local collieries, Griff Colliery. It was named "Lady Godiva" and used to raise water into the canal from a stream flowing underneath.

Britannia Bridge

WALK 16: WARWICK WALKABOUT
Distance: 5 miles

Parking: St Mary's Area 3 car park at the north end of Warwick Race-course.

This walk takes in canal towpaths, the River Avon and Warwick town centre.

The Walk

OS Explorer map 221 (Coventry and Warwick)

▶ Start by walking towards the end of the racecourse car park and go left crossing the racecourse towards the clubhouse of the **Warwick Golf Centre**.

▶ Go up the slope to the left of the clubhouse and after that go right taking a wide green track between golf course and driving range. In about 300 yards, cross over the racetrack and go through a kissing gate on to a footpath by a modern housing estate.

▶ Continue ahead through a wooded area and at the corner of the wood go right through a kissing gate on to a lane and descend to the road.

▶ Go left along the pavement beneath the railway bridge, then left through a gate onto grassland by the **Saltisford Canal Basin**. Follow the towpath and a grassy area passing a large narrowboat mooring area. Pop in to the **Visitor Centre** and have a look at the interesting photos of how the canal was restored.

▶ Continue along the towpath to the bridge and then climb up the steps to the canal bridge on to the pavement beside a road. This is **Budbrooke Road**. Do not cross over the bridge. Instead, go right along the pavement and in 50 yards you will come to a junction with the **A425**. Cross the road carefully going left over the canal bridge which goes over the **Grand Union** canal.

▶ On the far side descend to take the tow path into Warwick (about 1 ½ miles). There are several things to notice on your journey along the canal. Firstly you will pass under bridge 50 and then immediately under a brick bridge – also 50! You will pass canalside apartments on your right and then the **Cape of Good Hope** public house right by the first locks.

▶ Continue past another set of locks and bridge 49A. At the back of

Saltisford Canal

the hedge here you'll see houses on your left. You then pass under a footbridge by small industrial units followed by more houses to both right and left.

▶ Pass under bridge 49 and you will see **Kate Boats** on the right, with boat repair bays and marine services.

▶ Pass under bridge 48 then shortly under a footbridge and bridge 47. You will notice you are close to the town now.

▶ Continue under bridge 46 and the canal bends to the left with Tesco fuel garage to your right.

▶ Continue a very short distance to the aqueduct over the **Avon**. Just before the aqueduct, go left down signposted steps to join the 'Riverside Walk', turning right at the stream.

▶ Go right under the aqueduct and follow the riverbank footpath.

Julie M Chiswick   91

The first part of the walk is quite heavy with foliage and then you will pass under a metal railway bridge. Soon after this you will pass houses to the right. After this the riverside track soon opens out on to a grassy path in front of houses. You will find the riverside path becomes much more open as you emerge by a rowing clubhouse on the right and a footbridge on your left. You are now entering the grounds of **St Nicholas Park** and here the river appears wider and more pleasant to walk along. The first glimpse of the castle can be seen in the distance to the right. There are numerous benches along here if you wish to sit for a while.

▶ The walk soon leads to **Castle Bridge** and just after the boat hire place you climb steps on to the pavement of the busy A425. Cross carefully if you wish to see the wonderful view of **Warwick Castle** from the bridge.

Warwick Castle

Then turn around and follow the pavement towards the town. In about 200 yards go left and meander down **Mill Street** with its old well-kept buildings and at the end is another view of the castle.

Mill Street

▶ Return to the main road and pass the gates of the main entrance to the castle. Go round the bend into **Castle Lane** and walk through **Stables** car park into the grounds of the castle. At the far end, go through the archway past the café. There are toilets here if you need them.

▶ Walk through the second archway following the sign 'Exit to Town'. Walk along a short distance and then bear right to leave the grounds via a walled gate. Opposite here is **Castle Street**. Stroll up here passing by **Oken's House**, a lovely black and white building built 500 years ago, which is now tea rooms. (Thomas Oken was a wealthy merchant and Mayor of Warwick).

▶ When you reach the **Tourist Information Centre** on the corner of the **High Street**, turn left and walk along High Street. (See footnote about diversion to the market square.)

▶ At the far end of High Street, you pass through the archway of the **Lord Leycester Hotel**. You also pass the **Lord Leycester Hospital** listed buildings (see footnotes).

Lord Leycester Hospital

▶ Go right into **Bowling Green Street** and in 50 yards turn left down **Friars Street** to head back to the car park on your right near the bottom of the street. Notice the quaintly named **Bread and Meat Close** as you enter the car park.

NOTE:
If you wish to spend more time in Warwick, the market square is full of cafes, pubs and restaurants as well as the shops. To reach this, turn right off High Street into Swan Street and continue a short distance to Market Place. Continue back to High Street to finish off walk.

WALK 17: MERIDEN AND THE THREE GREENS
Distance: 5.5 miles

The Queens Head is just off the B4104 as you go through Meriden.
Park in the pub car park. No charge.

Close to Meriden, this walk takes in three greens: Eastern Green,
Pickford Green and Flint Green.
These greens were once areas of common land that mainly disappeared
under the Enclosures Act.

Julie M Chiswick   95

The Walk

OS Explorer map 221 (Coventry and Warwick.)

▶ Opposite the car park you will see a flight of steps leading to the main road. Go up these. Cross over the road to pick up the **Coventry Way** opposite. Go through a metal kissing gate and then in a few yards, a wooden kissing gate.

▶ Cross the field keeping to the left and you will soon see the tower of **St Laurence's Church** ahead of you. Go through another wooden kissing gate into the next field heading towards the churchyard. Stop to have a look at the church if it is open. There are many interesting features inside.

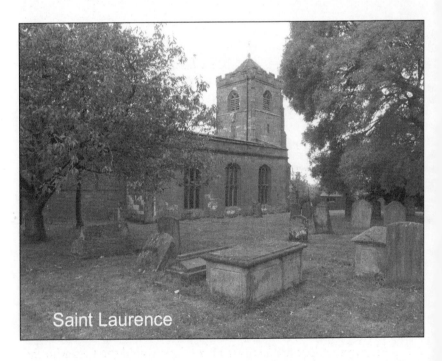

Saint Laurence

▶ Exit the churchyard to the left by a Coventry Way marker. You will join **Church Lane** and opposite is an old timbered building – **Moat**

Moat House Farm

House Farm. Turn right and walk past the church and **Church Farm** next to it.

▶ At the bend in the corner of Church Lane look for the signpost for the Coventry Way. Enter the field on the left by a gap at the side of the gate and follow the path through the field as it heads towards the hedge line on the left and a waymarker post.

▶ Keep the hedge on your left and the next marker is just to the right of the field corner. Continue with the hedge on the left to cross a wooden plank into the next field.

▶ Head diagonally left to a pass an old stile in the corner with markers. Continue through the gap slightly uphill with the hedge on the left. Cross through a metal gate. If the field is heavily ploughed here, stick to the right hand edge and continue round the field with the hedge on your right. Partway round the top edge, go through a wooden gate into a paddock leading to a house.

▶ Go left round the edge of the paddock and at the end of the fence go through a kissing gate in the corner and follow the access track and forward down a gravel track to the road. This is **Back Lane**.

▶ Continue left on Back Lane for about ¾ mile passing **Oddicombe** on the left and then several other houses on the left before passing **Greenways Farm Shop** and **Woodlands Farm** further on. This area is **Flint's Green**.

▶ You will see **Shirley Lane** next on your left but continue on the road. Just before a roadside pylon you will pass another farm shop and soon after **Oak Farm** on your left.

▶ About 10 yards after passing **Barnacle Farm** on the right, look for a public footpath on the left. Cross the stile and follow the track. This opens into a large field. Continue with the hedge on your left to a wooden plank bridge and cross the stile.

▶ Veer 45 degrees to the right to follow the path across to the hedge corner, to the right of the school. **St Andrew's Church** can be seen from here. You are now in **Eastern Green**.

▶ With the hedge on your right, cross a stile on to an enclosed path. Go forward to reach the road. This is **Manderley Close**. Turn right at the end of this on to **Church Lane** passing the social club and village hall on your left.

▶ Cross over the main road and go straight into **Upper Eastern Green Lane**. Walk along here for about 200 yards and after a small supermarket on the right, turn left between the middle of four apartment buildings. The kissing gate is just to the left of garages.

▶ Go through the kissing gate and then with the hedge on the right go through the field to a metal gate and across a wooden walkway. Cross the field to a gap, but if the field is heavily ploughed, go round the right hand edge to the gap. Keep the hedge on the left to the bottom of the field and follow the field round to the right.

▶ Turn left over a footbridge. Go forward. Pick up the hedge on the left and go up through a series of kissing gates bearing left until overhead power lines at the outward hedge corner.

▶ Cross the field to a pylon, go through a kissing gate and then diagonally left across the field to the corner. Go through the kissing gate, then down steps to the road. This is **Pickford Green** and the lane is called **Pickford Green Lane**.

▶ Turn left up the lane and then right at the junction with **Pickford Grange Road**. Continue to the next bend and at the end of the houses turn left down a track towards **Pickford Grange Farm**.

▶ Just past the farm and farmhouse, go through a metal gate to the right of a field gate and continue along the right edge of the field. Keep the hedge on your right and go through a kissing gate left of a field gate.

Continue slightly downhill. Keep the hedge then on your left towards two footbridges in the corner. DO NOT CROSS either of these.

► Turn right with the brook on your left over the next two fields. Cross the stile and sleeper bridge to continue over the next field with the brook initially on the left. Follow with hedge on the left round to the right until a kissing gate is reached near **Millison's Wood.** Go through this.

► Follow round the edge of the field with the wood on the right. Keep going round leaving the wood behind and with the hedge on your right you will soon see a metal gate between the hedges. Go through this. Turn immediately right, with the hedge now on your right and continue to the end of the field. This last field joins a farm track and then you go through a metal gate left of a field gate.

► Follow the track towards a farm with the church tower in the distance. As you approach the entrance to the farmyard, you must go right to follow the permissive path (signed). Keep round the edge of the farm and the bottom of the field. To the right of a house you will see the access road to Church Lane.

► Follow this and turn right into Church Lane immediately passing **Alspath House** on your right and then **Meriden House** on the left.

► At the main road, cross the road to **Old Road** and head back to the Queen's Head car park which is about 100 yards away.

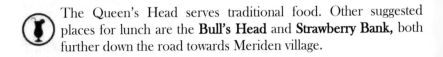

The Queen's Head serves traditional food. Other suggested places for lunch are the **Bull's Head** and **Strawberry Bank,** both further down the road towards Meriden village.

WALK 18: OVER WHITACRE
Distance: 4.5 miles

Furnace End is on the B4114. Park in The Bull car park (opposite the pub). No charge.

The walk starts from Furnace End and uses part of the Centenary Way as well as public footpaths and roads. It passes a Grade 11 listed building (Hoar Hall) and then Hoar Park Craft Centre. It is a rural walk and quite peaceful. There are some gentle uphill stretches.

Julie M Chiswick   101

The Walk

OS Explorer map 232 (Nuneaton and Tamworth)

The Bull

▶ Turn left from the car park, walk up to the crossroads and then turn right up the hill. After about 200 yards and after the end of the last house on the left you will see a marker to follow. It is right by a 50mph sign. This is part of the **Centenary Way.**

▶ Go through the metal gate and follow a rough grassy track at the edge of the field to the next gate and marker. Go straight across the edge of the next field with the hedge on the right. Exit through a metal kissing gate in the corner.

▶ Turn left and continue. At the bend in the road and just past a cottage, turn right at the public footpath. Go by the right hand side of a wooden gate to follow a grassy vehicle track.

▶ As you reach a gate signposted for Fisheries, you must take the kissing gate to the right of this and follow the edge of the field with the hedge on your left. At a break in the hedge you will get a good view of the large fishing lake.

▶ Continue ahead and through a metal gate keeping to the hedge line in the next field. Look out for lots of pheasants and quail darting out of the hedgerow here! In the right hand corner you will see a farm gate with a sign for Permissive Path. Ignore the metal kissing gate and if the farm gate is locked, go five yards to the right of the gate to a wooden stile.

▶ Follow this track between wooden fences. Look left to get a good view of **Hoar Hall**- a grade 11 listed building. Follow the track round to the left to a metal gate into the farmyard.

▶ You should pass another pond on your right as you go through the farmyard, bearing to the right and following the footpath arrow. At the

Hoar Hall

end of the last barn, go through a metal gate by the next arrow into a field.

▶ Head diagonally upwards across the field into the top corner to the next waymarker post and pick up the Centenary Way again. Go over the stile by the post and take care as there is a bit of a drop down on the other side.

▶ Follow across the field keeping the fence on the left. You are fairly raised here and look down to a long row of trees on the right and **Holt Hall Farm** in the distance on the left.

▶ At the end of the tree line you will see the next stile ahead of you by a hedge. Go over the wooden stile, then plank and then another old wooden stile into the next field. You will see Holt Hall Farm clearly on your left.

▶ This field is huge but you need to continue straight across heading for the edge of a hedgerow and keeping the solitary tree on your left as you walk across. Unfortunately, the farmers do not always make the routes easy by covering the fields with grass or crops!

▶ Continue ahead when you reach the hedge – with the hedge on your left. In the distance on the right you will be able to see **Hoar Park Farm and Craft Centre**.

▶ At the end of this field and just into the next field you will see the yellow marker on the right hand side. Go over the wooden stile. If you can, go straight across (without crops), to the next marker on the far side. If it is too difficult, then walk right round the edge of the field until you reach the marker. This is now a public footpath and not the Centenary Way.

▶ As you cross the stream with the craft centre ahead, you turn immediately right and head uphill on a gravel track to meet the craft centre car park at the top. Here you can stop for coffee if you wish. There are toilets and several craft shops if you want to have a short break.

► Make your way out of the craft centre heading towards the main **Nuneaton Road**. Turn right at the road for about half a mile until you reach **Monwode Lea Lane** on the right immediately before the large bend in the road.

► Go down the lane and you will pass a few buildings and then **Jasmine Cottage** and **Lea Lane Farm** on your right. The lane ends and goes into a track. Shortly after this go left after the metal gate.

► Follow the right hand tree line of the field. (At the time of writing there were earthworks here.) So follow the track round the edge of the earthworks to the right. You will eventually come to a gap in the hedge on the right.

► Go across the field to a waymarker. In the distance you should see the spire of **St Leonard's, Over Whitacre**. That is where we are heading. If the field is full of crops walk around the right-hand edge to the marker.

St Leonard's

▶ Turn through the gap and head down and across the next long field with trees and then a hedge on the left. You will pass a marker on the left. Go straight ahead, past a telegraph pole and towards a small barn.

▶ There is another marker by the wall of the barn. Go immediately left at this marker. There may be crops in this field, but the path is actually straight across heading towards the church and a yellow marker.

▶ At the marker, go through a small copse, over the stream and stile and on to a farm track.

▶ Go straight across through a metal gate and uphill to St Leonard's. The gate is to the left of the church.

▶ Exit the churchyard on to the main road. Cross over the road, turn right and head back to **Furnace End**. At the crossroads, turn left.

The Bull is on your left. The pub serves lunch up to 3pm at the time of writing.

Points of Interest:

St Leonard's was built in 1766, early in the reign of George III, in an Italian classical style typical of the period. However, it is thought this is not the first church built on the site.

Hoar Hall. The house was acquired by a member of the Weston family in 1692. Sometime around 1732 the house was rebuilt. The Weston's coat of arms appears in the central bars of the fanlight above the front door.

Hoar Park Farm and Craft Centre. The 141 acres Hoar Park dates back to the 1430s, the house and buildings dating back to 1730. These traditional farm buildings form the centre of the park and have been converted to house the craft centre and garden centre.

Hoar Park Farm and Craft Centre

Julie M Chiswick

WALK 19: DRAYCOTE WATER
Distance: 5.5 miles

Draycote Water is signposted on the A426 from Dunchurch. Park at
Draycote Water Visitor Centre. Charges apply.

The walk is around a reservoir and through gentle countryside taking in
an alpaca farm and the outskirts of Thurlaston village.

The Walk

OS Explorer map 222 (Rugby and Daventry)

▶ Exit the car park, walk up to the reservoir by a gate signed **Visitor Centre** and bear right following the tarmac path along the top of **Farnborough Dam** to reach the part known as **Toft Bay.**

▶ Towards the end of Toft Bay you will pass a small fenced garden on the right. At the very end of Toft Bay you pass a bird lookout on the left and shortly after a boardwalk on the left.

▶ At the sharp left hand bend in the road, you must go right, leaving the reservoir by a gate signposted **Dunchurch.**

▶ Continue ahead for about 30 yards and then go left up a small bank

Toft alpacas

to a gate and follow the waymarker signs. You will climb uphill past alpaca pens. There are lots of them and worth a photo!

► Continue along the track which then starts to go downhill. Go through a metal gate at the bottom and then follow the field uphill keeping the hedge on your left.

► At the end of the hedge go left through the gate, across a small piece of grass and head towards the gate opposite, in the direction of the little church. You will also see the mill slightly to the right.

► Walk along the lane and look to your right to glimpse a good view of the mill which is now a house. This ceased to be a mill in 1924. Continue ahead towards the church. The church is **St Edmund's Parish Church** and at the far end of it the church house is attached.

► Go left by St Edmund's Church and via a gate down a concrete farm track to a kissing gate and footbridge to enter the path around Draycote Water once again.

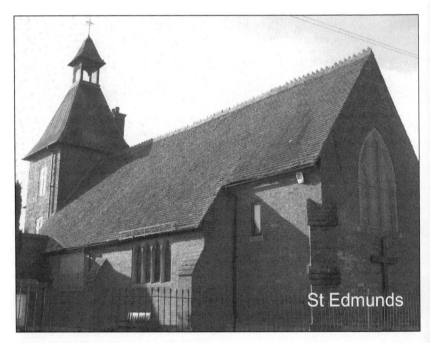

St Edmunds

► Go right along the path by the side of the reservoir eventually reaching **Biggin Bay** and **Thurlaston Grange** on the right and then past a golf course. There are several benches if you feel like sitting and enjoying the view or maybe even having a picnic.

► Continue round the end of the reservoir passing the treatment works and then along **Draycote Bank**. To the right you should see the spire of **Bourton-on-Dunsmore** church.

► Just before the yachting area, you will see a signpost for **Hensborough Hill**. Go right through a kissing gate on to a footpath that leads up to the hill. Look for the trig point and also the telescope. When you descend from here you go on a grassy pathway past the boats and Visitor Centre. You can leave here via a gate just by the Visitor Centre if you want refreshments or you can continue down the hill towards the car park.

Refreshments and toilets are available at the Visitor Centre. If preferred there is a pub - **The Dun Cow** - in Dunchurch village.

Thurlaston windmill

Points of Interest:

Draycote Water, owned and operated by Severn Trent Water, is a reservoir that supplies drinking water to Rugby. It was opened in January 1969. It covers more than 600 acres (240 hectares) and holds up to 5 billion gallons (23 million m³) of water. For a time the embankment was the second largest dam in the world - only the Aswan Dam was larger.

There are leisure facilities for sailing, windsurfing, fishing, cycling and walking.

Toft Alpaca Stud has a herd of between 150 to 200 pedigree Huacaya and Suri alpacas that graze on land adjacent to the reservoir. The animals can be seen close up and the stud runs a shop specialising in knitwear made from alpaca wool.

Draycote Water

WALK 20: CHARLECOTE AND HAMPTON LUCY
Distance: 6 miles

Charlecote is signposted from the A429. Park in Charlecote Park car park. No charge.

Some uphill stretches with beautiful views over Warwick and the surrounding countryside and an opportunity to visit Charlecote Park if desired.

The Walk

OS Explorer map 205 Stratford-upon-Avon and Evesham

► Exit the car park and turn right past the **Charlecote Pheasant Hotel** on the right and **St Leonard's Church** on the left, and go along the boundary of **Charlecote Park**, where you may see deer. In the middle of **Charlecote** village turn left down **Charlecote Road**, signposted to **Hampton Lucy.** After approximately ½ mile you see a public footpath leading to **Charlecote Mill** – a working flour mill open to the public twice a month.

Charlecote Mill

► Continue ahead on the road and go over the bridge spanning the **River Avon** close to the weir. Walk to **River Keeper's Cottage** gate and then turn left up a track inside a fence and going uphill. Go through a gate and continue on the track for a while. This is **Shakespeare's Avon Way.**

► At the next gate, emerge into a field and follow the track going right along the edge of trees. After about 200 yards you will see a gate (!) into the woods. Ignore this and stay on the bridleway at the edge of the field (the gated route is now impassable).

If you look left you may be able to see the **Welcombe Hills Obelisk** in the far distance. Continue straight ahead with the trees still on the right. As you get to the end of this field the path goes through a wide opening and as you go uphill you will see four oak trees in a row. There are good views to the right to **St Mary's Church** and **Warwick Castle**.

► 50 yards after the oak trees the path dips down to the right heading in the direction of a new farm building and house (house built 2015). As you descend you will see the public bridleway marker. Follow the track down to the farm. The grassy bridleway skirts round the bottom of **Copdock Hill**.

► Just past the farmyard make a 90 degrees turn to the left heading up the field towards a marker in the top corner. At the top you meet a small lane leading to **Wood Cottages**.

► Turn left on the lane and walk to meet the road at the end. Turn left again and after approximately ¼ mile turn right on to a driveway marked **Daisy Hill Farm** and **Daisy Hill Cottage**. 50 yards before the farm go left at a marked gate.

► Go across the field to a second gate and then turn right towards the farm. At the edge of the farmyard, you must turn left (through open farm gates) and continue ahead. The pasture descends to a wooden gate by an oak tree. **Clump Hill** is to the right. Continue downhill to a stile with the hedge on the left.

► Climb the slope uphill until the hedge turns sharply left. Turn with it and follow this bridleway with hedge on the left for about ¾ mile until you meet the road.

► Turn left along the road for about ½ mile and then right down a driveway, past a yellow marker to **Mount Pleasant Farm**. The path goes to the left of a barn conversion and at the electricity pole on your left you follow the track with the hedge on your left.

▶ Continue round the edge of the field and watch out for a stile by a gap in the hedge with a marker by electricity pole number CLFN4. Go over the stile and turn right. (You can see Hampton Lucy church as you cross the stile.) Follow the edge of the field with hedge on the right until you reach the road.

▶ Exit the field opposite **Tile Barn Farm** and turn left heading to Hampton Lucy. In about ¾ mile you will enter the village and see the **Boar's Head** pub, recently refurbished. While in the village it's worth a visit to **St Peter ad Vincula Church** – an interesting example of Victorian Gothic architecture.

St Peter ad Vincula

▶ Turn right at a road junction, recross the Avon and pass the mill once more before retracing steps back to car park. Refreshments and toilets are available at The Orangery restaurant in Charlecote Park.

Points of Interest:

Charlecote Park, built in 1558, has remained in the ownership of the Lucy Family, though the male line failed in the middle of the 19th century on the death of Henry Spencer Lucy. The Fairfax baronetcy, created on 14 March 1836 for Henry Fairfax, inherited the property and changed their family name from Ramsay-Fairfax to Cameron-Ramsay-Fairfax-Lucy to reflect the traditions of Charlecote.

Successive generations of the family have modified the house, which, although Elizabethan in origin, now has a mostly Victorian appearance.

Charlecote Park has extensive grounds, covering 185 acres backing on to the River Avon. It is rumoured that the young William Shakespeare poached rabbits and deer in the park, although it is uncertain as to whether there were any deer in the park at that time!

Charlecote Park gatehouse

WALK 21: ILMINGTON AND ITS DOWNS
Distance: 5 miles

Ilmington is a Cotswold village about 8 miles south of Stratford. It is signposted from A3400 or A429. The Howard Arms pub is in the centre of the village and has free parking to the front and rear.

The walk climbs to about 800 feet along an old drovers' road with stunning views. On the way a pool is passed. It is known as Newfoundland Well and is fed from a chalybeate spring discovered in 1681.

The Walk

OS Explorer map 205 (Stratford-upon-Avon and Evesham)

▶ Start the walk from the **Howard Arms** car park. Turn right to pass **Vine Cottage** next to **Kyte Cottage**. Between them you will see a narrow footpath. Follow this path which winds by the back of gardens and houses to a lane. Turn left and walk a short distance towards the school on the right.

Howard Arms

▶ Immediately before the school, go through the old kissing gate (erected for Queen Elizabeth II's Coronation in 1953) and follow a fenced way round the edge of the school to a stile at the end leading into a pasture. From now on the path across the fields is well signposted. Go straight across the pasture to the kissing gate and then on to the next one on the far side. Keep ahead in the next large field to another kissing gate.

▶ After this one you must go left to a further kissing gate partially hidden in the bushes. You will be following the arrows all the time. Here you will see the pool on your left known as **Newfoundland Well**. To your right are stunning views on a good day over parts of Warwickshire, Worcestershire and North Oxfordshire.

▶ The path climbs the slope beside a left hand hedge. Ignore any paths over stiles to your left and drop down to the next kissing gate. Follow the narrow pathway which is part of the **Centenary Way**. You will see an interesting house across the fields. Here the path goes down to a brook with a small lake to the right. Go through the kissing gate at the bottom and walk left round the edge of the field, close to the grounds of the house. The path goes uphill to meet a wooden gate leading on to the driveway of the house. Walk to meet the lane at the end of the drive.

▶ Turn left to start the climb uphill. This is about 1 ¼ miles steadily uphill past **Lark Stoke**. About halfway up you will pass a driveway signed **Upper Lark Stoke** and you will see **Stoke Wood** in the distance. As you near the top you will see a building tucked down on the left and a bridleway just after this. Ignore this one and continue to the top to reach the radio masts. By the masts you will see another bridleway marked on the left. Take this and walk between the low stone wall on your left and the hedge to the right.

▶ Pass through a gate into the next field and with the huge oak tree on your right, continue down to a gate on to the lane. Turn left and then at once right and follow the vehicle drive shown as a bridleway. You will pass two more masts. Here you are walking across **Ilmington Downs** and **Nebsworth Hill**. The path will skirt the edge of a wooded area. After about ½ mile you will continue ahead passing by a 5 bar gate. This section is an unmade track called **Pig Lane**. It can be a bit muddy at times. It is thought it may have been used in Roman times to connect **Ricknield Street** and the **Fosse Way**.

▶ When you reach the bigger lane, turn left and then after about 300 yards, take a signed path on your left. The path crosses the field to a stile. Continue downhill and then bear right at the bottom to a 7 bar gate. Go through this and follow the wide track which soon leads to **Grump Street**. On the right you will pass **Crab Mill** – a private house built in 1711 and a Grade II listed building. It was once an inn and three cottages.

Crab Mill

▶ Go past the cottages and descend past **Upper Green**. On your right notice the old Catholic church which is soon to be made into a village community shop (March 2015). At the junction by the village hall, turn right along the road which leads back to the Howard Arms.

 On the way you will pass the **Red Lion** on the left. Refreshments are served here or at the Howard Arms.

Points of Interest:

The parish church of **St Mary the Virgin** dates from the middle of the 12th century. Its bell tower has five bells cast by Henry Bagley of Chacombe in 1641, in addition to three bells added later.

Robert (Mousey) Thompson (whose work can also be found in St. John's in Berkswell) carved the pulpit and pews. He also carved his signature mice in eleven places throughout the building.

Ilmington Downs
The downs boast the highest point in Warwickshire at 858 feet. There are lovely views of the surrounding areas.

Ilmington Downs

11365414R00074

Printed in Great Britain
by Amazon.co.uk, Ltd.,
Marston Gate.